Through the Woods and Over the Hill

The Aging of America's Warriors

Bridget C. Cantrell, Ph.D.,

To order additional copies of this book and bulk quantity orders contact:
Bridget Cantrell, Ph.D., LLC
1050 Larrabee Avenue Suite 104, PMB 714
Bellingham, Washington 98225-7367
(360) 714-1525 or
www.BridgetCantrell.com

DEDICATION

To my late father, Charlie Smith Cantrell, Jr. United States Navy: World War II & Korean Conflict. To my precious mother, Carmen who reminds me always how much she loved my father and how handsome he was in his sailor uniform in 1945. To my little brother, Charlie Bill who never ceases to amaze me. To my beautiful daughter, Alayna who leaves me in awe. To my faithful felines, my steadfast steeds: Steqao and Maddie and finally to Sadie and Dottie my two Aussies who sit nearby as I ponder these words. Last but certainly not least a heartfelt thank you to my closest friends and veterans who have supported me in bringing the words of this book alive.

In Gratitude,

Bridget Cantrell

THE DESIGN OF THIS BOOK

It is common for most people to experience a sharp decline in eyesight as they grow into the senior years. Since this book is intended for you, the senior veteran, we have given careful thought to its text design and structure. We have chosen a 12 pt. Century Old Style type font because it is one of the most readable. Along with making sure the material is as simple as possible (keeping clinical terminology to a minimum) and speaking directly to you, we also have made an effort to ensure that our readers are comfortable in their reading adventure by producing it with larger and brighter text. Thanks for coming along for the ride.

TABLE OF CONTENTS

FOREWORD

by Lt. General Russel L. Honoré

Sacrifice and service on behalf of your country is more than a time marked in years alone. It offers a lifetime of learning and knowing of how to make the most of what you have and prepare for the many challenges you will likely encounter in your future.

After 37 years of uniformed service for the U.S. Army, I learned and experienced different models of leadership that prepared me for many hard times ahead. During these years, I witnessed the value of planning your approach, learning survival techniques and gathering information as essential to making decisions and taking charge of your life.

In my book, *Survival: How a Culture of Preparedness Can Save You and Your Family from Disasters*, its message of watchfulness, analysis and responsibility are drawn from some of the keenest lessons I learned during my service that easily translate from military culture to civilian life. Coming to grips with the inevitability of aging is not for the faint of heart. Approaching this time in our lives is all the more reason to begin planning and learning how to assess the situation, develop perseverance and engage life in a meaningful way.

I became acquainted with Dr. Bridget Cantrell when we were called to offer our comments on CNN and speak to the tragedy surrounding the shooting at Ft. Hood, Texas in 2009. In this new book, Dr. Cantrell speaks to what I have learned throughout my life and that is without preparation and precaution, you will be ambushed by the aging process. From my perspective, why wait until aging happens, you can prepare yourself by drawing from the strategic lessons for survival that you learned in Boot Camp, to expect the unexpected. Begin by knowing your strengths and weaknesses, trust the professionals for your care and respond to your life with eyes wide open. Throughout my career, I have successfully led teams as they faced seemingly insurmountable challenges and my final words to them and to you the reader, are see first, understand first and act first.

About Lt. General Russel L. Honoré

After four decades of uniformed service in the U.S. Army, General Honoré is best known for his role as the Task Force leader who mobilized the emergency management forces in the aftermath of the devastating destruction left by Hurricane Katrina in 2005. Lt. General Russel L. Honoré is a senior scientist with The Gallup Organization and the Preparedness Contributor for CNN. Today, Lt. General Honoré is retired from the military but he continues to speak on the topic of the culture of preparedness.

The General is a proud native of Louisiana and hails from Pointe Coupee Parish. As a highly decorated officer with numerous distinguished service medals including three Bronze Stars, Lt. General Honoré was awarded the Omar M. Bradley "Spirit of Independence" Award for his role in the recovery of New Orleans and he received the key to the city of New Orleans on the third anniversary of the city's recovery.

Lt. General Honoré holds a Bachelor of Science degree in Vocational Agriculture from Southern University and A&M College. He also holds a Master of Arts degree in Human Resources from Troy State University as well as an Honorary Doctorate in Public Administration from Southern University and A&M College. His new book, *Leadership is the New Normal: A Short Course,* was published by Acadian House Publishing in October 2012.

PREFACE

"I walked off the battlefield in one piece and said to myself, 'Okay...I made it' but never expected to live past thirty either. What I didn't count on was making it into my 60's and sure as hell wasn't ready for all the stuff that comes along with living so long."

Living through it; then living through it all to the end. Both ideas have their shortcomings when it comes to the aging process.

Time after time I hear veterans say they never expected to survive their combat experiences. Yet, to their surprise, they lived through what seemed like certain death and came out the other end with an unexpected extension on life. In the moment they had already prepared themselves to die, and almost like stepping into the afterlife, they found themselves miraculously continuing to live. The shock of still being alive after such harrowing events can easily throw one's life off kilter. For some, the bewilderment is no more than a minor bump in the road that flattens out over time. However, many veterans find it more than a distraction and the impacting turn of events can seriously mark their journey.

As a result, they continue on in life shadowed by an unsettling of mind and emotions because of those past happenings and, like any stressful experience, if it is not processed thoroughly it tends to get worse with time.

Because I am a mental health counselor my doors have always been open to the veteran community, and as a result I have many elderly veteran clients. These aging warriors have found their way to my office seeking to sort out some of the repercussions of that time in their past and most have never talked to anyone about it since it happened. They have tried to stuff it away out of fear or embarrassment that they would be misunderstood or found out. However, stuffing never works. As years pass, aging veterans struggle to confide in others about the difficulties in life following these events. Not only was the experience almost surreal but it gets compounded by the various debilitating effects of post-traumatic stress disorder from which many combat veterans suffer. Like those impacted by the stress of PTSD (who avoid talking about their experiences), aging veterans have found it difficult to talk about living longer than expected. These are veterans traversing the latter stages of life and feeling inadequate and unprepared for what they are presently encountering. In my practice it is not uncommon for a middle-age warrior to say that he never expected to reach this phase of life and the unforeseen extension on life has created much unexplained confusion.

So with these two thoughts in mind, never expecting to survive combat and then not foreseeing (or preparing) for the possibility of becoming a senior citizen after the war, are at the core of this book. The title, Through the Woods and Over the Hill is a play of words in the title of the Thanksgiving poem written by Lydia Maria Child. In any case, within its pages hopefully I've addressed some key issues (and possibly given some worthwhile answers) to the manner in which older veterans are handling life situations as they traipse through the woods and overcome obstacles while growing more mature.

As always, my primary hope for this book is that it will be of some benefit to those who take interest.

Bridget C. Cantrell, Ph.D., NCC, CTS

"I am young, I am twenty years old; yet I know nothing of life but despair, death, fear ... What do they expect of us if a time ever comes when the war is over? Through the years our business has been killing—it was our first calling in life. Our knowledge of life is limited to death. What will happen afterwards? And what shall come out of us?"

Erich Maria Remarque—*All Quiet On the Western Front*

1.

The Older I Get ... An Act of Surrender

There comes a time in every warrior's life when the aging process reaches the tipping point and for many a sudden, unexpected, window of reality opens confirming that life has a beginning and an end. The strong individuals that have made up our military forces over the decades will always see themselves as guardians of freedom and the protectors of the weak and helpless. So when nature runs its course and those resilient heroes of the past now find themselves the ones being helped and protected, it can become a stunning fact to live with. As much as their hearts want to go on in the role they have had since military service, the aging process has become undeniable. It then becomes time to make a life choice, "Do I refuse assistance and continue to make my own way or do I concede and accept what is offered to make my remaining years positive, productive and comfortable?"

To begin with, why do some warriors refuse assistance and do everything they can to "make it on their own" in the first place? It is mostly because of habits formed during their years of training. Training for military service has always been a life-altering process and, for the most part, certain aspects of that training become entrenched forever in the psyches of the young people that plow through it. A classic example of this is the memorization and adherence to the Military Code of Conduct. This code becomes a center point of military life and is ingrained in the very fiber of a warrior's consciousness. It is part of every test and inspection in the military and trainees cannot expect to pass their requirements or be allowed privileges (such as furloughs and passes) if they do not know this code inside and out. It becomes a conditioned mindset that was useful while in military service. The exact wording has changed over the years but it is still a mandatory component imbedded into every warrior's being. For the sake of clarifying the point I am making I will extract some wording from the Military Code of Conduct used up through the Vietnam Era.

In Article Two the subjects of "<u>surrendering</u>" and "<u>resisting</u>" are approached. They include:

2. *I will never surrender of my own free will. If in command, I*

will never surrender my men while they still have the means to resist.

3. *If I am captured I will continue to resist by all means available. I will make every effort to escape and aid others to escape. I will accept neither parole nor special favors from the enemy.*

Looking at these commands it is little wonder that so many veterans attempt to remain rugged independent individuals—convinced they can take care of themselves, in other words... self-reliant. They are the masters of their own ship and still conduct themselves according to a training regimen from the past. To accept the simple fact that they are elderly (aging has now become the enemy) flies in the face of this Code of Conduct. To accept that reality is subconsciously surrendering (an admission of their vulnerability, which is clearly not part of the Warrior Ethos) and they must resist (refuse help) as long as they can. This is not a positive thing and wastes a lot of energy that can be used to find peace within themselves.

No person, including veterans, wants to admit weakness and getting older indicates some forthcoming frustration in ordinary life situations. It does not have to be the burden that many think it is though; and my first suggestion is to take it a step at a time when coming head-to-head with this transitional issue. It can be a physical, mental or emotional challenge or consideration of where you are in life, so test the water before jumping in. Don't be afraid to try out new things and give what is offered a chance to work. You can then evaluate to see if it is right for you. This is a great way to work on changing your outlook about surrendering and resisting. Remember, not all shoes fit the same foot. We all take different walks in life. When a path is obscured by an obstacle, we must forge through it and navigate a new route. That choice is yours.

Coming into the senior years for anyone has its own peculiarities. Most people in their latter years find more suitable designations to refer to themselves rather than being identified as an "old" person. I'm not sure if it's a fear of being labeled something that would denote frailty or vulnerability or that perhaps we (I use "we" because I'm getting there myself) have just gone into the unsung agreement with political correctness. In any case, we, as a society, inherently avoid any undertones of being called an old man or old woman. In many ways that is not such a bad thing as I see it because I want to believe that we have earned respect and have wisdom and life experience as elders. However, some people make a concerted effort to avoid where they actually are on their life journey and they do this because it is too much like giving in or giving up. For veterans that can be like surrendering. Also when you accept the benefits and support society has to offer seniors, this may seem like an admission and classify you as "getting old". When that happens the Code of Conduct kicks in [I will accept neither parole nor special favors from the enemy.] and you find yourself refusing valuable assistance that can make your life better and easier for everyone—including your family that wants to care for you.

These are rights and privileges for which you were willing to sacrifice your life for as a young warrior and you should now enjoy the harvest. It is much like an old Middle Eastern metaphor of the ox pulling the huge grinding wheel at a gristmill. He is always allowed to eat the grain he is grinding out. In other words, by your service to this country you ensured that many benefits were intact and available for others. Now it is your generation's time to reap the benefits you fought for. I encourage you to consider accepting them graciously without feeling the least bit reluctant. Your military routines were important to adhere to at one time but some of them need to be revamped as you approach new horizons for living in this day and age.

As aging veterans you are at a place to recognize where you are, to acknowledge the price that was paid and then accept what you deserve. You no longer have to stick to an old mindset from military training (i.e. Military Code of Conduct). It will only mire you down and hold you back from the good life you earned. (I should qualify that statement by saying that I know from personal experience how important it was for my father to maintain the many good habits he developed during his years in the Navy. He learned work ethics, manners, respect, hygiene, responsibility and how to care for himself and those entrusted to his care. He brought that out of the Navy and translated it into making many good things happen for our family. That's not what I am talking about when I say "mired down and held back from a good life"; what I am saying is that some things just don't translate from military to civilian life very well. It is to your great advantage to look closely, recognize the mindsets and make the positive choices.)

You have the wonderful gift of choice. You can choose to see the glass half full or half empty and you can choose to hold onto old meaningless attitudes with a closed tight fist or hold everything with an open hand with the palm down. You can choose because you fought for the freedom to do so and it is your right.

2. The Strong Survive

For veterans, the law of the jungle (that the strong shall survive and the weak get eaten) has a deeper meaning than for most of us. In the realm of competitive business, when corporate takeovers are part of the scheme of things or an employee is systematically cut out of their job so someone else can get ahead in the game, it is said to be adhering to "the law of the jungle"…the strong survive. But this ugly brand of jungle ethics exists in a completely different venue than what combat veterans have known.

In every aspect of their training, veteran warriors have always been expected to be strong enough to survive life and death situations. That's what it's all about. They train to be successful on the battlefield where they must aggressively seek out the enemy—and kill him. The warrior then must not miss a beat in pursuing another victim to do the same. He does this until there are no more adversaries in his path. This is far from what corporate America or sports teams do to accomplish their goals. The "killer instinct" that is so energetically thrown around in football locker rooms and sales meetings in corporate America becomes a very real instinct to soldiers in the heat of battle. Without this instinct, the warrior is very lucky—or very dead. At any rate, every person who serves in the military will always have a different reality on the subject of "the strong shall survive." But when the once capable body and mind begins to decline with age, it suddenly is easy to feel more vulnerable and challenged by what were once ordinary life circumstances.

"Don't get hurt," the young man yelled at Steve as he took center field.

It was a hot Saturday afternoon and Steve had come upon a sandlot hardball game at a park near his home. He went home to fetch his mitt and then asked if he could play. The young players silently took a vote nodding at one another and Steve could tell they were not too excited about him playing. He hadn't heard that warning ("don't get hurt") in a long time. Not since he was five-years old when his mother watched him scramble up a tree in the park. Now as a man that had been through the woods of life it shocked him to hear those words. Even though he was in his fifties he simply didn't see himself any older than the boys he was playing ball with—until that moment. It was eye-opening, heart-rending and a defining moment that sent Steve spinning into a state of depression that would engulf him for the next few years.

Steve was a Marine during the Vietnam War and had

always considered himself tough and ready for action. He was someone able to accomplish any mission and to endure any pain and any hardship that may come his way. He did not receive the remark in the spirit the young man on the ball diamond delivered it. It was intended only as a reminder for him to be careful. Steve only heard, "Hey old man, we're not going to slow the game down because of you, so watch out because we play hard and you'll get hurt if you get in the way." He took it as a personal affront that challenged his manhood and instantly resolved to play as if he was nineteen-years-old again. As a result, not far into the first inning he turned an ankle going after a line drive—a play he would easily have executed some thirty years prior. As the younger players rushed to Steve writhing in pain on the ground, he refused their outstretched hands to help him up and struggled to his feet on his own. He hobbled off the field and headed for home to nurse his ankle—and his bruised ego.

It was the first time he had publicly come face to face with the limitations of his age. I say "publicly" because privately for some time now Steve had become aware of his changing capabilities and it was easy to shrug it off when he was in the privacy of his home or driving alone in his car. But now some of it had been put on display for others to see; and maybe make judgments about him as a man. I suppose one could say it was publically humiliating. They could perhaps question or evaluate, his personal qualities and attributes which appropriately classify him as a man—especially his physical strength. I have known many Marine Corps veterans throughout the years and of all the branches of the services the Marines come out of their training the most confident of their physical capabilities. It was a tremendous jolt for Steve to find himself waning and wavering with age.

For the many veterans that never expected to live into the golden years, being seen as an old person can present some stressful effects. Old age easily suggests that a person has become weak, vulnerable, susceptible, helpless, exposed and at risk to themselves and those around them. While as youngsters they went off to war feeling impervious to danger (dying was always for someone else) and because of their training they felt invincible. Getting old contradicts that reality and they don't really want to believe it but there is no other choice in the matter as nature is in control. It is easy to see how being classified in the "senior" bracket of society can create additional frustrations for aging veterans. Suddenly the reality of a senior discount at Denny's is more than a cheap meal…it is the reality of the aging process and unfortunately perhaps…a rite of passage.

My advice is to avert many of these frustrations by taking it one step at a time. Perhaps go back and use some of your military training to make the needed adjustments for a more fulfilling life as a senior veteran. Since Steve completely misread the young ball player's comment in the account above and only heard what he was feeling, it is a good idea to begin with some "observation training". Remember the observation course or the games the military used to improve your observation skills while in the field or combat? The idea is to be tested on "what did you see?" (What did you see compared to what is actually there or the perception we have conjured up in our minds.)

The training game went like this: The training cadre would put different objects on a table: a bullet, a paper clip, a bottle top, a pen, a piece of paper with something written on it—10 to 20 items. You and the other trainees would gather around the table and the cadre would give you, say, a minute to look at everything. Then you would have to go back to your table and describe what you saw. You were not allowed to say "paper clip" or "bullet", you would have to say, something like, "silver, metal wire, bent in two oval shapes." They wanted you to report only what you actually saw. Another one is to have a cardboard box sitting on a table in front and you are asked to describe what you see and then questions are asked along the way, like. "How many sides does this brown object have?" If you answered "six" you are assuming that is a whole box but because you cannot see all the sides and you are relying on assumption according to your previous knowledge base, you are wrong. The box may not have a back, side or bottom…you are not observing what is actually visible, you are answering according to what you "think" is there, not what you are actually seeing.

In the case of Steve "hearing" the young man say "Hey old man, we're not going to slow the game down because of you, so watch out because we play hard and you'll get hurt if you get in the way"; He assumed the boys were thinking and saying the worst about him and this became the source for his agitation. Had he utilized the observation training he could have possibly avoided the frustration. Had he stopped, taken a deep breath and observed what was happening, he may have discovered that they genuinely did have his safety in mind…or he could have at least taken the time to see it from their point of view before going any further. Even if he was not sure of their intentions (possibly they were being mean-spirited about it) he could have still chosen to go by the actual words spoken…which were, "Be careful don't get hurt" and believe the boy meant it. Instead, Steve made matters worse for himself by going on mere assumption that the boys were ridiculing him because he was older. These were video tapes that ran through his head and they essentially rendered him at a disadvantage simply because he began questioning himself which took him off target.

It is so important for you as a senior veteran to make good solid observations in your decision-making. If you do the natural adjustments from young to old it can all be made within your comfort zone. Remember, relying on and reverting back to some of that good old training of yesteryear is a very sound (and simple) idea—one that you have some familiarity with. Try it out and have some fun.

3. The Age Ambush

O ne of the blessings of our creation is the built-in safety feature of not knowing when our lives will end. Of course there are always some cases where circumstances, such as health issues, can give us an idea of approximately when that time will come but even then the exact moment and second remains a mystery. I suppose this is why executions are so terrible; to be able to count down the time increments from life to death is a cruelty that none of us were meant to endure. So we wake up each day and go on with eternity in our hearts, never spending much time contemplating the fact that it will eventually happen. It's just our human nature not to think about it much and that's why when something does go awry and lives are abruptly ended, it comes as such a surprise. Likewise, when we suddenly awaken to the fact that we have reached a place in life where it is not as easy to perform as we once did it is then we get ambushed in a big way. So, after consulting with some veteran colleagues on the subject of "ambush" I will use that concept to illustrate some of the elements surprise as we grow older.

When that "tipping point" on the seesaw of life reaches the other side of the balance and it begins to tip downward, it is at that juncture we discover, perhaps for the first time, our limitations due to the aging process. Many veterans get hit heavily with the element of surprise when it happens.

Being caught off guard is one of the primary stress factors (it is a trigger) that plague combat veterans all their lives. In my practice I see it every day and have become attuned to never "springing" anything new on my veteran clients without alerting them that something is coming. I am very careful to always give reasonable and logical advance notices of any changes, whether it be in our conversation, the change of décor in my office, therapy times, topics, etc. I take extra care when I am called out of town to speak or provide counseling. I let them know that they can still contact me and/or that we will have an appointment set up upon my return. I simply do everything possible not to "ambush" (surprise) them. It is the unpredictability and disruption in routine that can throw them into a downward spiral.

If you recall within the standard definitions of an ambush, the element of surprise becomes the all-important component... and without it an ambush cannot be achieved. Here is a short definition for you:

An ambush is a long-established military tactic, in

which the aggressors (the ambushing force) take advantage of concealment and the element of surprise to attack an unsuspecting enemy from concealed positions.

In keeping with our topic of aging, the chief enemy is time. It seems to keep itself hidden from us and many times catches us flatfooted by showing up in the form of a malfunctioning mind and body. You may still think of your body as the strong young unit with arms, legs and feet that once propelled you easily over an obstacle course and through a hot jungle to reach an objective but now it is protesting the climb up a few steps. And overnight the law of gravity has seemingly redesigned your build into something resembling …"an old person"! That is the ambush in force.

Making it into the golden years contains its own element of surprise for those warriors never expecting to reach thirty. When they suddenly experience some of the limitations and disadvantages (which are mostly physical) it comes as a real shocker. It is the ambush that has been sprung—and it is important to know how to break its power by going on the offensive. Offensive action is the only way to break through an ambush…it is never a defensive attitude that gets you out. We will outline some ways that can be done

A number of consequences can follow the sudden impact of becoming aware of limitations encountered with age. Since we are paralleling these sudden realizations (of advancing age) to an ambush, let's carry through by using similar nomenclature and illustrations. Once again I want to thank some of my veteran friends that have taken the time in helping me illustrate some of the military descriptions and jargon.

I will first give an explanation of a standard military ambush sequence and then parallel that with comparisons to the aging process. Then and most importantly, I will offer some ways to ensure some "damage control".

So here we go.

The key components of an ambush are as follows:

Planning

Ambushes are complex, multi-phase operations and are, therefore, usually planned in some detail.

First, a suitable killing zone is identified. This is the place where the ambush will be laid. It's generally a place where enemy units are expected to pass and which gives reasonable cover for the deployment, execution and extraction phases of the ambush patrol. A path along a wooded valley floor would be a typical example.

This Translates as:

The various stages a human body goes through during a lifetime are multi-phase processes. There is little to compare with the immense complexity of our anatomy. The vital systems (skeletal, muscular, cardiovascular, digestive, endocrine, nervous, respiratory, immune & lymphatic, urinary, female reproductive and male reproductive systems) however, are not designed to last forever. They will break down with age and eventually cease to function.

While in our youth very little attention is ever given to most of our anatomical systems and functions. On the most part; these hidden but essential elements exist on auto-function for younger people and not much thought is given to them on a daily basis. Not many in their younger years begin making a plan for the inevitability of old age aside from perhaps saving money and making long-term financial investments. The signs of aging in the mirror's reflection or physical pain and the limitations of age, remain the wakeup call for most of us—but that seems to always come many long miles down the road.

Since our various systems are obviously as temporary as life itself, not enough can be said about the importance of each individual's responsibility in nurturing what we have been created with. As we mature and signs of the eventual breakdown begin to surface, we may begin to recognize the changes and most of us start adopting lifestyle changes to ensure that the closing stages are as trouble-free as possible (this is a good way to stay out of the ambush "kill-zone" in the first place). Good food/vitamins, exercise, rest, relaxation, spiritual nourishment and proper medical care all combine to provide an enhancement in our happiness and health. Like so many aspects of human individuality the adoption of healthy regimens and sticking to them are a matter of choice and some miss for far too long. Human nature, combined with our inherent free-will, can serve to work against us and not everyone is going to bother with taking positive steps in maintaining healthy regimens. If we don't take heed and reject the right choice, we will likely step into the proverbial "kill zone" much faster than others of our same age.

Preparation

To be successful, an ambush patrol must deploy into the area covertly, ideally under the cover of darkness. The patrol will establish secure and covert positions overlooking the killing zone. Care must be taken by the ambush commander to ensure that fire from any weapon cannot inadvertently hit any other friendly unit (this is known as crossfire).

This Translates as:

For some of us age comes on slowly and does not reveal itself all in one shot. It shows up in photos that someone takes when we least expect it. Or the barber cuts your hair and more grey is revealed. Or the stairs you have always easily run up suddenly seem too long and steep. The age ambush takes us by small surprises much of the time. I have talked to many older veterans who say that in their minds they are still operating as if they were that teenage kid that could run faster than a speeding bullet and leap from tall buildings with a single bound (later we have a chapter dedicated to this phenomenon). Most veterans have this eternally-nineteen-year old syndrome and age sneaks up on them in the form of an array of limitations or heaven forbid, injuries due to the mind compelling the body to act like it was still as pliable and strong as it once was. By not preparing for the eventualities and taking the needed precautions, aging warriors can become victims of their own ambushes. Don't skip all those stair steps and slow down. Don't leap that ditch on the golf course, walk to the bridge. Life is better when you aren't immersed in nursing a sprained, bruised or swollen body part.

Waiting

Having set up the ambush, the next phase is to wait. This could be for a few hours or a few days, depending on the tactical and supply situation.

This Translates as:

Time is the enemy when we speak of the aging process and the primary weapon of time is the element of waiting. In an ambush or firefight situation in combat the objective of the aggressor is to pour continuous firepower into the ambush kill zone. This action has all been made possible because they have taken advantage of waiting for just the precise moment to deliver the most damage. As the recipient of this onslaught we too must take advantage of the element of waiting…but just in reverse. We should not wait at all! As the enemy shows itself we should not lie down in the kill zone or try to hide the fact that we are where we are in life. The standard practice for an infantry unit to break through an ambush is to do everything possible to go on the offensive. Return as much fire as possible. Move as fast as possible. Never go on the defensive and succumb to what is coming at you—if you do there is little chance of achieving any satisfaction of your own in the process. When you notice that paunch in the mirror, don't procrastinate…hit the gym at your own pace but decide then and there to lose some weight and enhance your condition the best you can. Don't prolong making that dental appointment—no matter how inconvenient or painful you may think it will be. We may only have a certain amount of time on this earth but we can step out and take positive steps to capture the good things that will make us happier and healthier along the way. Don't wait. I always ask my young warriors and veterans alike, "Who understands the importance of time more than a warrior?" To them a moment in time a life can be lost and time is something we can never recapture. Time is of the essence, so take heed, go forth and use it to your advantage.

Execution

The arrival of an enemy in the area should be signaled but the enemy must not detect the signal. Some military doctrines call for an ambush to be initiated by a signal from a whistle, though in US practice whistles are not favored since they do nothing to inflict damage on the enemy.

This Translates as:

We begin to get signals of our advancing age all through our lives; from the arrival of teeth in infancy to pre-teen pimples, to adolescent voice changes and menstrual cycles. "The beat goes on" and the whole world around us witnesses these changes. No one escapes these signals and every phase of our growth has its telltale signs. Probably our biggest mistake is to not make ourselves aware of the signals when they do go off and then get caught flat-footed with the unavoidable changes taking place. I will reiterate my observation that getting caught off guard is one of the key components of stress issues for veterans. Preparedness is crucial for every warrior I've met and when time begins to overtake the strong individuals that have prided themselves in fearlessly protecting the weak and innocent, it can become an ordeal of great magnitude. I encourage you to watch the signs carefully and heed the call to accept and adjust the inevitable changes that are happening to you. It is the only way to break through the ambush. Warriors never want to be caught flatfooted, they want to keep their edge sharp, so this is a chance to hone your skills of observation and tune into reading your body more accurately so you can re-evaluate what your objectives really are.

Surviving

By definition, the ambush contains the element of total surprise; which means the victims of the ambush have no knowledge of how it has been constructed or of what measures may have been employed to prevent escape. Therefore – and this has been proven by the experience of war – the only likely method of survival is withdrawal from the killing zone "the way you came in". The value of withdrawal is the preservation of the force to "live to fight another day".

This Translates as:

With modern technology and advancements in medicine we are more aware than ever of what it takes to remain healthy. So, through this tremendous base of knowledge the intricacies of how the "ambush" is constructed gets revealed, thereby giving humans the advantage over the aggressor called "time". It brightens us with ideas and the effective means by which we can traverse the zone (called life) with much less suffering. To preserve our health we must strive for balance in all things: Mind, Body and Spirit. The following are simple principles to help you make the journey and survive with good health and happiness:

1. Maintain proper rest, relaxation, exercise and diet.

2. Develop your spiritual connection with that which gives you meaning and purpose.

3. Avoid substances that are proven to damage your life: Addictions: Drugs, Alcohol and Unhealthy Food.

4. Using your training of observation, detect in advance most stressful situations—and avoid them. Don't get ambushed.

5. Consult regularly with trusted doctors, fitness coaches, dietitians and physical therapists...including massage and energy experts.

6. Fill your time with enhancements; always seeking to improve yourself. Set personal goals, fulfill dreams and remain hopeful.

7. Last but not least, discover the wonderful world of giving. Your experiences have provided you much to share with others. Do some volunteer work at something like the local USO for example. You give of your time and experience and expect nothing in return. The benefits and rewards are out of this world...literally.

4.   Nineteen Forever

My body came home from Vietnam but my soul is still there. It feels like I'll be nineteen forever and I just can't get out of that frame of mind."

It is so common in my practice to hear these words. It's almost as if the impacting experience of going to war, especially an unpopular war like Vietnam, has created what movie-makers call a "freeze frame." The teenagers deployed during that time period now find themselves partially (or sometimes wholly) frozen within a mental video of the past. They came home believing that everything would return to normal…to be as it was before they left. As hard as they hoped and tried, little was ever the same again. Unlike the troops of today, there were no pre-deployment/ post-deployment briefings or de-briefings, so each young warrior created his own reality (fantasy) of how things would be when it was all over. When the ensuing life scenarios did not conform to that reality, the veteran established many self-improvised ways to cope and make sense of where he was and now is. In that process he found himself living in the now with his mind primarily still in the combat zone of yesteryear—and to make matters worse, he kept the dilemma to himself feeling that no one would ever understand or believe his story. So many of the Vietnam veterans shut down, even hid out and lived off the grid, thereby avoiding the challenges of trying fit into a society that had little compassion or desire to validate their pain. That generation of warrior created their own reality and found others who had similar experiences in the war to surround themselves with.

There is much to the old adage, "young and impressionable." Everything about going to war impinges greatly upon the psyche of young people and creates lasting impressions. Since it has always been an agreed upon consideration that war is best fought by young people, it is the young that are lined up and marched off to face the horrors of combat. It is no wonder that the word "infantry" derives from the word infant, which got its start far back in ancient times. Back then an army would go to war and the small boys were trained and commanded to run alongside the cavalry horsemen armed with spears, clubs and other simple hand weapons. If they survived and lived long enough to become older warriors they qualified to join the cavalry and then could mount a horse and ride into battle.

An infantryman is known as a "grunt", a self-explanatory title, because an infantryman walks (and walks and walks) into battle carrying heavy loads of weapons, ammunition and survival equipment. He is a beast of burden that must also have the stamina to fight effectively once he arrives upon the scene of battle. This is not a job favorable for older people and you can see why. As a result young and impressionable warriors are marched onto the fields of glory and deeply affected by their experiences. They then carry the war inside their hearts and minds for all time. Because those mental images are so deeply ingrained, the young warriors' psyches become fixed in place within the freeze frames of those long gone youthful years. Those old impressions, however, do regularly re-surface in everyday life, causing the acting out to be akin to the actions of a much younger person— this is being "nineteen forever." Here it behooves senior veterans to remember how the ambush works and do everything possible not to get tripped up this way. Keep in mind that your actions or the lack thereof, will impact the loved ones in your life and may lead to misunderstandings that create more hurt feelings. Know where you are in life before making any responses.

Over the years, I have seen veterans that are out of sync with themselves and their environment just because they are still expecting (or demanding) their bodies to keep pace with their minds. Don't get me wrong, I truly believe that feeling one's age can be dictated much by our attitude and feeling young in mind is a good thing. All I am getting at is that by adopting preparatory measures and giving some forethought to pairing (synchronizing) our mind with our body you can avoid much unnecessary pain and frustration. I also know and have seen this in many veterans that come through my doors for help, that when the aging body has been victimized by a youthful mind, the injuries are a reminder that we aren't what we used to be. Many times this results in a degree of melancholy and could even lead to full blown depression if left unattended. Knowing yourself is important, as well as knowing the difference between what your mind is telling you and what your body is capable of. This is the best way to stay on full alert and ready for more good things to come. As I mentioned before, balance in our lives is vital and having realistic expectations means adjusting the view of ourselves. We have a tendency to reminisce about our youth, our strength and even laugh about how crazy and omnipotent we felt in those younger years. I see this a great deal with veterans; they speak as if it was just 24 hours ago when they were young warriors and were dodging bullets or out on operations. I know that for most who served our country it is often the most important time and significant life changing event they have ever seen.

My friend and writing colleague, Chuck Dean, is a veteran of the Vietnam War. He is now a senior veteran and over the years has written several books to help veterans with readjustment issues. He began writing in his early forties, soon after discovering that he was suffering from Post Traumatic Stress Disorder. (It took him fifteen years after returning from the war to make this discovery, which is not uncommon.) In his first book written in 1987, "Nam Vet: Making Peace with Your Past" he mentions his own encounters of being out of sync. The following is an excerpt from the book. I think you will appreciate some of his observations and discoveries:

"A real eye-opener caught up with me a short time after I began working with Vietnam veterans. In my search to find other vets I was unconsciously looking for guys in their twenties, strong and in good shape. The movie Platoon had just hit the local theaters and it gave me a golden opportunity to seek out fellow vets. I stood at the door of the movie house and tried to identify the veterans in the crowd. As the theater emptied out I would zero in on someone with an Army field jacket or a camouflage shirt or hat but quickly learned that these weren't the clues to look for. Instead, I had to check for the graying beard, the slight pouching around the waist and the deep creased lines on the face caused by years of alcohol, drugs or prevalent worry. When I realized I had been looking for the wrong age group, I had to laugh at myself. My 'Nam Vet brothers were middle-aged (now elderly) and I hadn't noticed it until then! Though we still keep our teenage memories alive, we are not kids anymore.

"What we're up against now is old age...having gone

through mid-life change; this all compounds to make some interesting (and persistent) effects of PTSD. I don't have a background in psychology or psychiatry so I can't make any concrete pronouncements on the subject but a few laymen's observations may help someone who is more qualified to take this on as a study.

"During the period of a man's mid-life change for example, certain desires become the central focus, controlling his thoughts and actions with a nearly overpowering influence. It is a time when masculinity appears to be at a turning point. The man looks in the mirror and wonders, "Am I still the man I used to be?" He may begin to wear teenage clothing styles, gold chains around his neck, unbuttoned shirts that allow his chest hairs to be fully seen and more fashionable hairstyles. His attention goes to driving sports cars or "something with flash," so that younger women will notice him. In short, he attempts to revert to years when he was a virile young man with no worries and with strength to take on the world. He also reverts to "toys" (motorcycles, boats, etc.) and actions that identify him as a young stud on the make.

"If this reversion syndrome is a substantial trait of men in mid-life crisis how does it affect the Vietnam veteran?

"Not long ago, I was in Canada and met a veteran by the name of Gavin. (There are nearly forty-five thousand Canadian vets who served in the U.S. Armed Forces in Vietnam.) He was a clean-cut executive-type with a tweed sports jacket and graying temples. He should have had a pipe in his mouth but didn't. Gavin told me that recently he had the sudden urge to buy an M-14 rifle like the one he had used in 'Nam.

"We had quite a laugh about his urge. But then he told me he had purchased the weapon and found great pleasure in shooting it. Was it PTSD or mid-life crisis that caused Gavin, a most unlikely candidate, to develop this impulse to buy an M-14? I believe Gavin's experience was a mid-life reversion to a time when he felt that the only security he had was the possession of that weapon.

"I've known many veterans who have bought army field jackets, jungle fatigues, insignia and all the assorted paraphernalia when they got into their middle age. And I've heard them say, "Well, what do you know...I'm finally getting some pride back, because now I want to wear my medals and uniform that I wouldn't wear when I got home." I believe the restoration of pride is part of it but I think that the strong mental pictures of youthful virility play a large part in their impulse to buy these items as well.

"At an age (seventeen, eighteen, nineteen years old) when the adult mind is still developing, we had our lives interrupted. Our adult personality developmental process came to a halt for nearly an entire year and the only thing that mattered then was survival. This disruption caused many unresolved problems when we tried to resume normal life as young men. Now that most of us are in our middle age (now sixties and seventies) we have the additional issues of dealing with our senior years. It is time to deal with our teenage PTSD and get it into remission so we can have the peace we deserve in our latter years."

I think Chuck's advice is very sound. He writes from a veteran's perspective that I'm sure you can identify with. Be a student of life; take time to explore your relationship with yourself, your past and how this all relates to your present situation. Change has occurred and it is an opportunity for growth and to see yourself from a different vantage point.

Ambush Escape Route Reminders

1. Synchronize your mind with your body. Slow your body down so your mind has plenty of time to be in command of every possible situation.

2. If you are caught off guard and sustain a physical injury that serves as a wake up call that signals, "you're not as young as you once were", don't shrug it off without fully processing it. Seek out trusted counsel and talk it out. (Remember, stuffing is never a good thing and doesn't work for long.)

3. Know who you are and where you are in life.

5. A Family Affair

At one time there was a statistic that indicated the issues plaguing every Vietnam veteran will impact nine other people in their life. I believe this to be much more and not only for Vietnam veterans…but all veterans.

It is evident that in today's tightly connected social world we cannot avoid putting our stamp on other peoples' lives; what matters most (as the bottom-line) is to ask ourselves…are we affecting them positively or negatively? I would hope that everyone desires to make positive lasting impressions on those around them and especially those we care about and not the reverse. Most challenging issues in veteran family circles find their source in the matter of Post-Traumatic Stress Disorder (PTSD), which I discuss in detail in Chapter 6 of this book.

The stress a veteran carries into the family after experiencing the dreadfulness of war can make them hard to be with or live around. Living with someone who is easily startled, is self-medicating, has anger issues, nightmares and often avoids social situations can damage the most caring family. How does

PTSD have such a negative effect? It may be because those suffering with PTSD find it difficult to feel emotions or the emotions they sometimes feel are not appropriate for dealing with issues on the home front so they shy away from feeling much of anything. As a result they may feel detached from others and get further away from the very thing (relationship) which could help them lessen their emotional burden. They tightly batten down the hatches so they will not feel grief, loss, fear, sadness and so on. These are some of the feelings stimulating the painful memories of the past. However, by closing the doors to those feelings they also obscure the feelings of love, closeness, compassion and joy. The diminishing of such tenderness obviously can cause difficulties in personal relationships and as an older veteran I'm sure you have seen your share.

Likewise, over the years your family may have been hurt, alienated, fearful, and/or discouraged because of your stress levels. I know I looked up to my father who suffered from PTSD all my life and I couldn't help but wonder why such a strong, independent man, was not able to overcome the effects of his trauma in the war. I found out why later but it was still a difficult thing for a young girl to live with for so long. If this is the case in your family, be encouraged though…it is never too late to change some things—hopefully the material in this book will give you a new understanding to help make those changes.

As for me, when I was a young girl I experienced many emotional rollercoaster rides as I witnessed first-hand the aging process of my father who was a WWII veteran. From youth to adulthood, growing up with him put an indelible stamp on my life. In retrospect I can see that living with him gave me much first-hand knowledge of how our veterans bring the war home with them. Those lessons learned have become invaluable in my life and practice. For instance, I became aware of how much it affects the entire family to have a loved one go off to war and then return with a different perspective on life. Living with my father also taught me much about the intricacies of helping veterans and their families when it comes to dealing with re-adjustment issues. As a wonderful by-product of that, I have developed a great sense of compassion and empathy for our warriors and their families and have a keen sense of how important our job on the home front really is. It simply comes down to the honor of loving our veterans and showing them the deepest level of respect for their sacrifice. I have much to thank my Dad for and my work with warriors and their families is a direct reflection of that.

From the time I was small all the way into adulthood my warrior father was always larger than life to me. He had a presence about him that made me feel loved and protected. However, at the same time I feared his anger. Even though he was very defending of our family he could, at any time, surprise us with the "shape up or ship out" or "my way or the highway" bit when things got out of his control. Consequently, we toed the line because we knew he meant it. When those moments occurred in our family, none of us ever suspected that it had anything to do with his military service. Only after I began to educate myself on the matters of war stress did I realize I had been a living example. Looking back I know that he was being reminded of something stressful and dangerous and he wanted to make sure that we did the right thing in order to avert an unsafe situation. I loved my father for being so careful to defend us. However, it did cause all of us to walk on eggshells more than we liked to.

One thing I discovered later in my practice is how much combat veterans love to drive themselves to the edge. By taking risks that pumps their adrenaline they subconsciously thrive on re-visiting similar feelings (highs) that they got from combat. When Dad would take risks it became a scary time for me. One summer he took us fishing out in the Pacific Ocean in a sixteen-foot ski boat. He was confident that he knew how to handle a boat in any kind of water but the waves became like walls around us. My brother and I were terrified as we watched Dad wrestle to control the boat in such high seas. He lived close to the edge and thought nothing of it when it was over; but to this day I know we were lucky to have survived.

Another example of this adrenaline high occurred near

our home in Seattle. There was a very busy road with constant traffic traveling at high speeds and we lived on a sharp corner that produced many accidents. On a routine basis we were always the first to the scene, assessing the injured, calling in the police, etc. Assisting the survivors until help arrived, Dad was in his glory. In the midst of the sirens, blood, broken glass, the smell of fuel, moaning—and even death, I could literally see the adrenaline surge in him. It was like he was back in a combat zone—and at his peak. He drew me there with him and I learned at an early age how to triage the wounded!

One Saturday, to get him out of the house and around veterans, I invited him to visit the Vietnam Wall Memorial that was traveling though our city. When we arrived I led him out to the black Wall. He stood gazing at all the names of those who had given their lives in Vietnam and then suddenly he whirled around with his cane in his hand and walked away. I slowly followed him as he left the park to make sure he was okay. Finally I sat next to him at a picnic table as he wept and said, "Coming here to this Wall not only represented the Vietnam veterans who were lost but all those who were killed in my war as well." The experience impacted him for many months afterwards but I knew something important had happened to him. Even though this hard experience opened an old wound it was a defining moment for him because at that point he began to honor his own service more than ever.

His heart was tender and wounded by the buddies he had lost in war and this brought it all back.

He had his health issues as he aged. He was a 6'2" long and lean sailor whose nicknames were "Legs" and "Sonny". He was strong and in my eyes there was nothing that my dad couldn't do or fix. He began to lose his height and put on weight. He was not as strong and agile as he once was and his loss of physical prowess and tenacity was difficult for him to accept. He tried his best to maintain that level of function but the aging process had taken over. He had fought many battles in his life and this was going to be his last. During 63 years of marriage my mother, Carmen, was there and always faithful. She is to be commended and honored for her tenacity and undying support that she gave us all over the years.

As he got closer to the end of his life Dad softened into a very loving man who was a gentle soul. He loved people and seemed to have more of those fun belly laughs. As he confronted the illnesses overtaking him he knew that his last chapter was coming to a close and one day he gently cradled my face in his hands and looked into my eyes and said "I feel that I have hurt you as a little girl, would you please forgive me?" It was a defining moment for me but little did he know that this forgiveness took place many years before he had ever asked. My upbringing brought me lessons about life and survival that I can carry forward to hopefully help other families understand how these challenges impact all of us.

My hero, my father and my best friend died in March of 2008. Charlie S. Cantrell, Jr. who enlisted in the U.S. Navy at the age of 17—before WWII broke out—was an incredible human being and it was through his service to our country that I have become the person I am today.

6.   Getting the Family on Line

Every veteran could make a list of what he or she needs or wants to make his family life more peaceful and comfortable. There are endless relationship scenarios and situations that can arise in every family circle. These can be largely magnified when everyone is struggling or coping along with you and your war stress. You must realize that you are dealing perhaps with your PTSD but your family is not only dealing with PTSD but with you as well. When this is happening it is time to make a plan and the first item on the agenda is to inform the family of what is going on.

When there is a person who is suffering from PTSD within a family the key to getting on track is education. Getting everyone on the same page is paramount for peace and healing. If this doesn't happen, I know from a lot of experience about the tremendous hindrance that crops up in reaching the needed solutions for a positive outcome.

Don't wait for your family to initiate…you are the one to do it. It is your experiences that everyone wants to understand, so you need to be the teacher for the family. As the helmsman and family leader, do everything you can to provide the family with reasons and answers for what has happened in the past and what is happening now. Your reactions to situations will be much more understandable and tolerance will be built by allowing your family into the window of your past. With that being said it is very important to know your audience and set boundaries on how much you choose to share. It is never too late for healing, even with families that have struggled in the dark for many years. I know this seems to be a daunting task but perhaps I can help.

Before we go any further on the topic of family education it is important to talk about "the wire". It is an essential piece of "secret" information that you possess and a vital part of the education a family needs. By explaining this phenomenon to them you will ensure they get the most out of understanding your behavior and reactions as a result of your experiences. I have written many times about this "wire", which is the emotional barrier that is subconsciously put in place by people who have come face-to-face with the horrors of war, conflict and disaster. As part of the education process I will explain and PLEASE encourage your family to take the time to read this section carefully. It will do much to bring peace to your home.

It goes like this:

For many young people who become service members, the first time they have ever loved anyone beyond their immediate family is the friends (buddies) in training and when they go to war. They became part of a close-knit military unit...and it is like a new family to them. They learn to love those to whom they entrust their lives. It is the witnessing of some of these close friends getting hurt that makes the pain so great, so they learn to avoid future pain by building their individual firewalls. The warriors exposed to such impacting events draw lines and string up perimeter wires to defend against future vulnerabilities. In other words, walls are built to insulate them from feeling the intensity of the pain they may have felt when their buddy was wounded or lost in battle. It all equates to a form of emotional self-preservation.

The firewall computes and tells them that it is best not to get too close to anyone—so up goes the "wire" around us. It now exists to keep us from feeling any more pain because we "know" we have had enough to last us a lifetime.

When the war is over there is a new twist to this phenomenon—our subconscious firewalls do not go away by just ceasing to fight. They remain in place and as advanced as our military has become, there is little in place to help a warrior become a person who can once again think, react and socialize as a civilian when their enlistment is over. Veterans are virtually thrust back into a society that can now be difficult to relate to anymore. This feeling of being an outsider further pushes them deeper behind enemy lines to where they feel they are not well equipped to advance toward their friends and families without getting more wounded.

Once back in the "real world" warriors are expected to be normal human beings again. As trained combatants we return firmly convinced that we will not allow anyone to cross over to certain points on our side of the wire. As a result we forfeit much intimacy and closeness with those who desire and expect it from us. Subconsciously we decide that if we did allow this crossing and if anyone got hurt on "our watch", it would be too much to bear. As a result we maintain a wide "no-man's land" between us and the rest of the world and so it begins—the emotional shut down, the separation, isolation and alienation.

So exactly what is the anatomy of the "wire"?

Sometimes, people find themselves in situations that can overwhelm them with helplessness, horror and fear; it is especially impacting when they find themselves in danger of losing life and limb. These events are called traumatic experiences. Some common traumatic experiences can include physical attacks, being in serious accidents, serving in combat, sexual assaults, proximity to traumatic loss of life, child abuse or falling victim to fire or natural disaster such as a hurricane. These all can dictate to a person that a wire must go up in order to lessen the impact or prevent painful emotions and memories that have a tendency to interrupt and interfere with our daily lives. After traumatic experiences most people will likely find themselves having some challenges that they did not have before the event. Moving away from that which is painful, whether it be physical or emotional, is a survival tactic but over a long period of time it can disrupt our lives to the point of being destructive and dissolving what means the most to us.

Most combat veterans fully expect to return to normal life after war but most seem to hit a brick wall after brick wall when trying to allow others to get close for the intimacy they desire. The obstacle here is the wire and it is one of the chief culprits that hangs people up in transitioning back to civilian life. It is, however, a method of self-protection not limited only to war veterans. When we describe "the wire" we find that people from all backgrounds express their familiarity with this mechanism. It is the duration of traumatic events for those who fight in a war that makes it so much more impacting and difficult to relinquish.

The wire helps us maintain comfortable distances. It is a necessary means of keeping us from being hurt again. What is important to hear is that it was never strung up with the intention of not loving anyone or being loved. However, it does exist out of the secret fear that those near us could also get hurt if we "authorized" them to come too close. So, "the wire" serves its purpose both ways in protecting those you love from further harm and you from deeper emotional wounding.

After trauma, this fear may dictate something like this: "If I let them come across to this side of the wire and into my heart, I could never forgive myself if something happens to them. I'm not sure I could endure the pain and anguish again like I had when my buddies got hit in the war." The next part of this mental computation is prompted by past trauma. It goes something like this: "It is better to keep them out and even if it means that I am alone—I will be responsibly alone on this side of the wire and I won't have to risk losing them again." Furthermore, "If I keep them at a safe distance they will never see the real pain that I am dealing with; they will never know and I won't be found out."

Summing it up, stringing up an emotional perimeter creates an invisible barrier used to keep others away. Sometimes this barrier is implemented through anger and aggressive tactics. So recognize this anger or emotion for what it is and get to the core of why you are letting it cause more problems in your life. Remember, it is in place to deny others access to the emotional suffering and pain that is imbedded in a warrior's heart and mind. It is the inner person saying, "I've had enough! Don't come over because I don't want you to suffer with me." I use the following quote by David O. McKay in all of my workshops and it pretty much speaks to the pain in the soul. "The most difficult of life's battles are the ones we fight in the silent chamber of the soul."

There is sometimes a deep moral conflict which also contributes to the decision of getting close to people.

The Veteran's Stress Points and Wish List

The following is a veteran's wish list. It is, by no means exhaustive. Simply use the list to get some ideas of what and how you can tell your family about your experiences. It will give them more information to help bring peace and harmony to your family interactions. Once you have read the list over try to add to it with some of your own particular stress points.

1. Ask them to provide you with space. Tell them: Sometimes I need to be alone–but don't take it personal. I only need to reinforce my perimeter because I have some special boundaries that I developed during the war and this helps me deal with stressors better.

2. Ask them to limit their questions about your past. Inform them that you will be glad to talk when the time is right. This is very important and these questions can seem very invasive and spark some sensitive memories.

3. Ask them to be patient with you; especially when you are irritable and remind them not to personalize the times when you may explode or want to be alone. Remind them that it's not them…it's you. At the same time be patient with them as well. They really do not understand.

4. Ask them to include you in conversations and decision making because you need that respect and involvement and you don't want pity. This is very important for you to feel connected and one way to do this is to be involved.

5. Ask them not to say "I understand" when you know there are some things that they cannot understand work together to find another word of acknowledgment. Be aware that sometimes the words "I understand" may be their way of conveying empathy.

6. Familiarize them with your anniversary dates (significant dates during the year that traumatic events happened in the past…dates that cause you to be "out of sorts" because of past events). Inform them about how this could be a tough time for you and to be aware. It is best to work together, keep communication open and fluid so they can assist in helping your transition through this difficult period but help them understand boundaries.

7. Remind them that from time to time that you want to be closer to them and share your feelings more but you hesitate simply because you sometimes do not know how to express your emotions. This can be because you have repressed emotions for so long as not to feel pain, this also trickles into your intimate relationships as well.

8. Remind them that you love them, even when you are

going through your highs and lows. Be sure to remind them that your moods do not affect your love for them.

9.   Ask them not to demand that you go to crowded and noisy places because it makes you uncomfortable and puts you on alert, work together to find a suitable activity in which you both feel safe and secure. There can be a variety of triggers which activate your hyper vigilance, so be sure to share as many of these triggers with your immediate circle.

For the Family - What Veterans Don't Want

The following are comments and misconceptions, which oftentimes do more harm than good when family members try communicating with their veteran. It is advisable to avoid them:

1.   Avoid telling a person who has gone through a stressful experience ("I understand right where you're coming from." or "I know how you feel."). If you have not experienced it yourself this falsehood could alienate your relationship. The person who has been traumatized may think you are patronizing them and minimizing their feelings of experiences.

2.   Avoid telling a person that he or she needs to "just forget about it, it will go away with time" or "Get over it!" because PTSD symptoms if left alone may worsen. By not talking about it and avoiding the subject does more harm than

good. If the veteran will not or cannot talk to you about the issues, help them locate an experienced therapist or support group of other vets if the veteran is comfortable talking about his or her experiences in a group setting. Veterans knowing that they are not alone and that they have another veteran who understands their experience is the beginning of acceptance and healing.

3. Avoid unwarranted labeling of people who suffer from PTSD by telling them they have a "mental illness". Remember that most people subjected to the emotionally negative impact of war will never be the same again. The experts say that PTSD is a normal response to an abnormal set of circumstances. The individual is reacting to life through the impressions of something that has taken them outside the range of a normal human experience. They have a new skill set and some of their reactions are actually survival skills that have brought them home. Our warriors are self-reliant and the last thing they want is to be labeled and stereo-typed.

In conclusion, it is good for family members and friends to remember that when their loved one left home to serve in the military they stepped out of one world and into another. In most cases they were thrust into a new environment overnight where they had to readily adapt and learn to survive with a new set of rules in unfamiliar surroundings. As a new soldier (sailor, airman or Marine) they had to strive to become a working member of this new life. In the process, they usually had to develop a new persona and identity within this new "community" setting. From day one of boot camp/basic training they began to change as they came under the iron hand of the drill cadre. Then came the tremendous personal danger and stress of wartime duty that demanded that all the good morals of peaceful living be thrown out the window in order to survive. If loved ones of a veteran can see and understand these concepts then they will have much more compassion, empathy and awareness to support their veteran. So start the dialogue and be present with your veteran, suspend judgment and honor them by giving them the opportunity to share their story, their strengths and challenges with you.

7.   The "Later in Life War"

As you may have already discovered, some things show up unexpectedly as you get older. Aches and pains where there were none before, sudden loss of mental or physical ability or feeling vulnerable to the environment you once controlled—or so you thought. These are common concerns for every person as they reach the senior years. However for veterans there are additional obstacles to overcome that are unique to them alone. I call this the "Later in Life War" because of the difficulties and challenges senior veterans now face as a result of their military service.

First and foremost is the subject of Post Traumatic Stress Disorder. If you are a senior veteran and served many years ago, you may find that your military experience still affects your life today. Memories of wartime experiences can still be upsetting long after serving in combat and there are a number of reasons why these symptoms of PTSD may increase with age but first let us explore PTSD a bit. For your comfort call it what you will: Combat Stress, Post Traumatic Stress, Soldier's Heart or even Battle Fatigue.

So what is PTSD?

A simple definition is that PTSD is an anxiety condition that is caused by an event or series of events that have threatened life or limb and it was an experience that goes beyond the normal range of everyday human life situations. It is seen in survivors of traumatic events, such as military combat, natural disasters and involvement in violence. The key symptoms after exposure to such traumatic events consist of: reliving the event, avoiding situations or interactions that remind one of the traumatic event, feeling numb, becoming depressed, lack of self-esteem or being emotionally or physically activated to the point of being quite sensitive and hyper aware of surroundings, finding it hard to sit still, let your guard down or quiet your mind. Since drugs and alcohol are a popular way to self-medicate some veterans use them to either numb themselves out, sleep or temporarily forget the upsetting past events. Veterans with PTSD may also have other issues including: feeling hopeless; lack of purpose or meaning and even questioning how they survived and others didn't, so there may be shame, survival quilt or despair. They may also have employment issues, unstable relationships and even physical symptoms that represent much of the anxiety they are dealing with.

Historically PTSD has been around for a long time but it has only been a subject of study for a relatively short while. It has an interesting history related to more modern warfare. Over the years, the symptoms have been widespread enough that it has been given various names. During the U.S. Civil War (1860-1865) it was referred to as Soldier's Heart. By World War I, it had been renamed Shell Shock. During World War II it was still called Shell Shock but then advanced into Combat Fatigue and was also called that during and after the Korean Conflict. For a short while during the Vietnam War it was known as Delayed Stress Syndrome and in 1968 it was officially re-categorized and given the current label of Post-Traumatic Stress Disorder.

There is much written and disseminated about PTSD and our modern military has the advantage of in-depth access to what it is they can expect by being exposed to danger and trauma as a result of their duties. So, for the sake of our senior veterans we will zero in on your particular issues and obstacles to tackle. We will also explore why PTSD symptoms tend to increase with age and become more noticeable. The following is a short list of some of the concerns older warriors may be challenged with:

- If you have retired from work your symptoms of PTSD may feel worse. This is because you have more time to think with fewer things to distract you from your memories. This is why hobbies, along with productive and interesting activities, are so important.
- You may have certain medical issues that are getting more

pronounced and more difficult to deal with. This may make you feel like you are not as strong as you used to be. This can increase symptoms and other mental health concerns, such as depression. This feeling of vulnerability brings to mind how life has changed and you are not as capable in certain areas as you used to be.

- You may find that bad news on the television, movies and scenes from current wars bring back painful memories. It is a good idea to be more selective when it comes to exposing yourself to programs or situations which may have a tendency to activate your stress. Knowing what your limitations and triggers are is vital to managing your life better.

- You may have at one time coped with stress by using alcohol or other substances. As you have aged you have now become more health conscious or physically ill or dependent. This is certainly something that needs to be addressed and dealt with aggressively. If you have ceased to drink or use drugs, which is great but you may not have replaced those old habits with healthier ways of coping and this is causing your mental health issues to worsen. There is most likely a void in your life and it is very important to fill this with a healthy mindset. Please be proactive with the self-medication and turn to other means to deal with your stress.

Many older Veterans have functioned well since their military experience and then later in life when things are not so intense they begin to think more about their past and become emotional about their wartime experience. As you age, it is normal to look back over your life and try to make sense of your experiences. It is as if you are doing an inventory and wondering if you did life good enough. There is also a grieving process that takes place when we realize there is a "letting go" of that hard driving young person; but gracefully accept that and realize you are growing into another phase of your life.

For Veterans this process can trigger what professionals are now calling Late-Onset Stress Symptomatology (LOSS). *(Aging Veterans and Post Traumatic Stress Symptoms, 2007, http://www.ptsd.va.gov/public/pages/ptsd-older-vets.asp)*

The symptoms of LOSS are similar to those of PTSD but with LOSS Veterans will likely have fewer or less severe symptoms. These symptoms, of course, appear later in life. LOSS differs from PTSD in that it is more closely related to the aging process and veterans with LOSS might live most of their lives relatively well. If they are still working they find it relatively hassle-free and they spend time with family and friends in a usual manner, with few upsets. But when they begin to confront normal age-related changes such as retirement, loss of loved ones and increased health problems, the stress begins to surface more and more. As they go through this stress they may start to have more feelings and thoughts about their military experiences. While some may find remembering their wartime experiences to be upsetting, many also discover that it helps them find meaning to what they lived through.

What can you do to find help?

If you are having a hard time dealing with your wartime memories, there are a number of things you can do to help yourself.

- Try to do things that make you feel strong and safe in other parts of your life, like exercising, eating well and volunteering. I mentioned the USO as a great way to volunteer because it is directly related to what is near and dear to your heart as a veteran. Of course there are other veteran organizations that have regular activities geared towards community service and veteran issues: Veterans of Foreign Wars (VFW) and American Legion are typical examples.
- Talk to a friend (preferably another veteran) who has been through the war or other hard times. A good friend who understands, listens and cares is often the best medicine.
- Consider joining a support group. It can help to be a part of a group of your peers who share similar issues. Some groups focus on war memories, while others focus on the

here and now. A good group that some of my veterans have made much progress in is one that focuses on learning ways to relax. Check with your local Vet Center or VA to see what they have going on in your area.

- Talk to a professional. It may be helpful to talk to someone who is trained and experienced in dealing with aging and PTSD. There are proven, effective treatments for PTSD and your veteran buddies, physician or clergy can refer you to a good therapist. You can also find information on PTSD treatment through the Department of Veterans Affairs and your local Vet Center.

- Educate your family and friends about LOSS and PTSD. It can be very helpful to talk to others as you sort through your long-ago wartime experiences. It will help to put them into the right perspective. Making these things known is helpful for those close to you to gain some insight on what may be the source of your anger, nervousness, sleep, emotional distance or memory issues. The more they know, the more they can provide the support you may need. This transparency and openness can set your relationship on a fresh new path to healing.

- Remember…it is only the brave who ask for help. There is no need to feel bad or embarrassed by asking for it—when you do ask it is a sign of wisdom and strength. Now set your sights in a positive direction! Doing nothing and hiding behind some of the painful, negative thoughts and behaviors does not serve you or your loved ones. One small step is the beginning of a new journey.

The Rocking Chair War

PTSD symptoms do not lessen with age as many would expect. The symptoms tend to worsen soon after retirement and the reason for this primarily is because you were submerged in the work force for many years. You stayed busy and could bury earlier experiences and thoughts about war trauma by throwing yourself into the world of business or competing in the work place. However, now that things have slowed down and you begin to search for things to do, you may find yourself reviewing old memories or contemplating the many roles you have been responsible for throughout your lifetime; especially in the military. Were you a leader of warriors and did you lead others into dangerous situations? Were you a good leader? If not a leader, did you have to follow bad leadership as ordered and did that leadership make errors that still frustrate you? Memories and thoughts about one's roles can be endless and now you have all that spare time to mull things over that you haven't thought about in many years. If you find yourself bothered by things that come up please be encouraged to seek out someone to help you sort it out. Don't let it silently stir and distract you from being relaxed and comfortable now that you have reached a place to do so.

Veterans at retirement age may also experience additional stressors as they step into a new world of adjustments. Slowing things down from a faster pace can be quite the challenge and the ambush has been laid in your path. You can make yourself so overly busy that you begin to neglect more important things such as personal health and family. Don't get caught up in this kind of trap.

Hopefully you have given this some thought and prepared yourself both mentally and physically to make the leap from working to retirement. However, even if you have prepared there are many pitfalls that can still cross your path.

One of those hazards goes back to realizing where you are in life. If you have not gracefully given yourself some advance "thought" to what will come as you age, you may be in for some painful surprises that possibly you can avoid by prepping yourself. Many senior warriors have come to me distressed over the passing of a friend to illness or even by natural causes. They had not given much thought to how they would feel when something like this happens. Now they are suddenly hit with the realization that they are getting older too—and so are their close companions. When this occurs, the loss and fear of loss has a tremendous impact on them.

The next issue is economics. To live on a fixed income or to live on declining economic resources takes some adjustment as well. If one is not prepared, it can cause some serious setbacks to your general outlook and well being.

Another prevailing aspect of the "rocking chair war" is that many elderly combat veterans that are troubled with PTSD are also burdened with physical pain and discomfort due to the stress. Stress can clearly lead to a downward spiral and this is why it is so important to know how to read yourself well. When illness strikes in the senior years it can be magnified in veterans by out-of-control worry and frustration, along with other stress-related complications. Since PTSD is an anxiety issue, it frequently affects the cardiovascular system, central nervous system, digestive system and endocrine system, which can cause chronic health conditions and lead to further challenges.

As advancements in medical miracles continue to develop and human life is extended, veterans will also live longer. PTSD in our warriors will undoubtedly become more prevalent and recognized as time marches on and the young warriors today fighting the global war on terror will someday be senior veterans themselves. It is my hope that some of what I am compiling here will be beneficial to them as well and the generations to follow.

The Veterans Administration (VA) is opening more care facilities around the country and always looking at a variety of treatment modalities to meet the various needs of our veterans. For example, some of the current treatments available for PTSD include: medication to help with sleep, nightmares, anxiety and depression; stress and anger management classes; counseling groups for PTSD and grief; and individual counseling with a provider trained in working with veterans. There are group counseling sessions available, some of which are specifically designed for older war veterans. At these group sessions you have an opportunity to share past experiences while gaining more understanding just by listening to the experiences of other veterans. There are PTSD treatment programs at numerous VA Medical Centers around the country. Some are for extended periods of time and really do offer some great support, education and normalization of what you are dealing with. The camaraderie that you will experience when you are in the presence of other veterans is extremely valuable. I highly recommend that you look into what your area offers. Knowing and caring about other veterans' war events can do much to increase your own healing. In the process you will learn how to support others in their healing from war trauma. It's a worthy goal indeed.

8. Reflections

It is rather easy to understand the financial costs of going to war but when it gets to the personal price that the warriors and their families pay it more difficult to compute. In war there are other prices paid that most of us are never aware of. War is more than sacrifice. It's even more than chancing death while facing enemy fire. The bottom line cost of war occurs when its participants are asked to go beyond the paradigms of normal life. Warriors train to kill and killing is the essence of war and that's the highest price we ask our brave military to pay. The aging warrior who has engaged in or supported for them unthinkable activities (that war, by its very nature, always calls for) has much to ponder and for the first time may begin to mull over whether their actions were right or wrong. These are the wounds of the soul. Coming to terms with some of these struggles is a difficult task and it requires speaking the words and telling your story. It is like lifting the burden from your heart and allowing someone you trust to share in your emotional pain. Please don't think you must do this alone; it is time to get all your affairs in order so you can live out your remaining years without suffering from what you may have lugged around for years.

During youthful years on military duty…especially while at war and for some years after the war…a veil of patriotic duty can protect a warrior's outlook on any sense of whether he (or she) was right or wrong. The vows made to uphold the agreed upon precepts of which our country was founded and stands for, overwhelmingly shadows any compunction to make moral judgments about his or her actions. At one time, within the young warrior's mind, those patriotic beliefs served as moral armor to keep them safe from self-condemnation. But that does not always hold up for veterans shifting into their senior years. Why? Simply because they have had more time to reflect on the rhyme and reason of their experiences. Although I must add for clarification, that these hard reflections do not, in any way, insinuate that their patriotism is waning or that they have developed doubts about their earlier commitments. They have simply seen more of what a complete life is all about and they now place more value (and thought) on the process of living instead of dying.

For young people, the meaning of life is framed by styles of appearance, language, material acquisitions and social affiliations in the quest for a solid footing in the external world. This quest for meaning, however, goes through a radical change once you come face to face with life or death encountered in situations like combat—no matter how old you are. This explains the disappearance of innocence that so many veterans say they lost while at war as a younger person. Herein is the dividing line between young people who have never been to war and those that have. The young man or woman that goes to war is faced with the difficult task of bringing meaning to the terrifying and brutal experience—they must in order to survive the aftermath. To maintain a reasonable degree of sanity after such chaos, young warriors need to find meaning by understanding the deeper levels of what they lived through. There really are no other options if one wants to have a fighting chance of adjusting properly after the war. The search for this meaning is the process that causes a person to mature more rapidly than others. However, those that haven't gone through war have the privilege of maintaining the option of growing at their own pace, experiencing all the developmental milestones into adulthood and putting this quest of meaning and purpose off for later or never—and some people never grow up at all.

As for older veterans, the search for this meaning undergoes a major shift in the second half of life. As we age, most of us find less and less meaning and value from material "things" and begin to look inward rather than to the outer world for the essence of life. It is a natural process that we all arrive at and participate in—one way or another.

I'm not certain that any of us can determine the exact meaning of our lives but it is in the seeking where the magic lies. Since after wartime experiences each warrior brings home something different within their heart and mind, they each have something distinctive to work on in the process of adjusting back to normal life again.

No two people are impacted by trauma in the same way and the inner and spiritual growth will occur magically when an honest effort is made to understand the many facets of their particular experience. But, I must warn you; for veterans reflecting back on wartime duties and actions (both intentional or unintentional) it can be a rough journey and just like the old "buddy-system", where nothing is done alone, you should not travel this road by yourself, at least not in the beginning. Once a supportive guide has come alongside and walked with you for awhile and you have made substantial gains in your search, then it may be time to step out on your own. It is important to put closure to some events in life and having a "battle buddy" who can support you through this journey helps smooth these transitions.

I am acquainted with one veteran who traveled many years alone and used writing as a means to debrief himself. He wrote endless notes to himself and burned them after writing them down. He would keep journals and describe his war experiences.

When each journal's pages were filled, he would conduct a private ceremony by going to a place in the forest to burn the journal. He said that it was his way of talking out his war experiences and bringing some closure. He had always felt that no one would ever understand what he was saying or how he felt, so he used writing as a way to cope with all the things he had stuffed and bottled up inside. Later in his life he discovered the relief of being part of a group of fellow veterans and the healing he got from talking to others who could relate to what he had gone through. This veteran initially used writing, which is a very personal and private expression, then moved into the process of actually sharing his story verbally with others who had similar experiences. This was the beginning of reconnecting with himself, then with others and eventually branching out into others groups of people with whom he may not have had the military link.

This brings me to mention and highly recommend, the amazing book *What It Is Like to Go to War* by Karl Marlantes (Atlantic Monthly Press August 30, 2011). Marlantes was a Marine officer during the Vietnam War who led other Marines into many extreme combat situations during his tour of duty. His writing proclaims the gut-level truth of combat and a very honest look at the repercussions that follow. It took Mr. Marlantes several decades after the war to begin to even think about publishing his private thoughts about war. I would like to include a small excerpt of this book that is significant to the idea of reflecting on your experiences and communicating about them in a quest for closure—and hopefully some healing. Here it is:

"I wrote this book primarily to come to terms with my own experience of combat. So far—reading, writing, thinking—that has taken more than forty years." (Marlantes, 2011)

"My feeling now? Oh the sadness. The sadness. And, oh, the grief of evil in the world to which I contributed.

"What is different between then and now is quite simply empathy. I can take the time and I have the motivation, to actually feel what I did to another human being who was in a great many ways like my son. Back then, I was operating under some sort of psychological mechanism that allowed me to think of that teenager as 'the enemy.' I killed him or Ohio did and we moved on. I doubt I could have killed him realizing he was like my son. I'd have fallen apart. This very likely would have led to my own death or the deaths of those I was leading. But a split [the separation of feelings from what the act calls for] occurred then and now cries out to be healed.

"My problem was that for years I was unaware of the need to heal that split and there was no one, after I returned, to point this out to me. That kid's dark eyes would stare at me in my mind's eye at the oddest times. I'd be driving at night and his face would appear on the windscreen. I'd be talking at work and that face with its angry snarl would suddenly overwhelm me and I'd fight to stay with the

person I was talking with. I'd never been able to tell anyone what was going on inside. So I forced these images back, away, for years. I began to reintegrate that split-off part of my experience only after I actually began to imagine that kid as a kid, my kid perhaps. Then, out came this overwhelming sadness—and healing.

"Integrating the feelings of sadness, rage or all of the above with the action should be standard operating procedure for all soldiers who have killed face-to-face. It requires no sophisticated psychological training. Just form groups under a fellow squad or platoon member who has had a few days of group leadership training and encourage people to talk."

No Solo Ops

In the many years that I have been counseling veterans, I have found that talking through situations, in detail—not skimming, is where the real healing lies. As Mr. Marlantes has illustrated so well, that "split" as he calls it, needs to have the feelings of the incident joined together with the actual events and details of what happened. There are many ways to heal that split but it still comes down to each individual human coming eyeball to eyeball with himself or herself; and much of this will show up when we share our experiences with others. This requires vulnerability and transparency where "the wire" dissolves and pretense is clearly not part of this experience. This new relationship with oneself is based on authenticity.

I'm reminded of a legend among the Cheyenne Indians and it goes like this: There was an isolated village on the edge of the forest. For years the people there practiced a routine. One by one they would sneak out of the village and follow a small path through the forest to a silver stream. There was a log over the water, which had been worn smooth by many moccasined feet. Looking around to make sure no one was looking, the Indians would walk out onto the log and look into the silver stream. In the smooth flowing water they would see their reflection. Then, in a quiet voice, they would begin to talk. They would tell the stream all the deep things of their heart. Doing this made them feel good and when finished they would return to the village.

Even though everyone in the village did this on a regular basis, they never told anyone. However, everyone seemed to know that everyone else was doing the same thing—but their pride kept them from openly discussing it.

According to the Cheyenne, the meaning of the legend is that everyone needs to relate with someone by telling them the profound things of their heart. But since sharing such things is also considered a sign of weakness, the Cheyenne dared not talk about it with anyone else.

The legend is half right. We humans are created with a deep need to relate and share our lives (especially our challenges) with one another. However our society has done a strange thing by conditioning us to think we are displaying weakness by sharing private and sensitive issues so openly. We see "success" as the ability to go it alone, to make it without anyone's help and living by the motto…never let 'em see ya sweat.

I must say that this is a struggle that is alive and well with not only aging veterans but with our active duty military as well. I personally know how important it is to share your concerns with someone you can trust. Perhaps a conversation is too lofty of a goal right away so write about it, participate in creative and cultural healing practices: connecting with nature, equestrian activities, movement, creating art, practices which support your spiritual or faith base. Create a ritual or rite of passage that helps you remain healthy in mind, body and spirit, with the objective of keeping communication open. Closing off from emotions and experiences can also result in more stress related illnesses. To have challenges in life is normal and it is our mission to find peace and balance by having a friend, a ritual or spiritual practice which helps us purge the pain and replace it with growth and a lighter heart.

American veterans have a strong sense of independence and for the most part are reluctant to ask for help. Growing up on a healthy dose of "rugged individualism" has set that idea rigidly in place. Yet, like the Cheyenne, when you are alone standing on that log looking down into the silver stream and there is a strong urge to speak the deep things of your heart—maybe even about the deep secrets of wartime trauma—it's okay, it needs to be done. That water signifies life and is carrying those secrets downstream. The only difference to that precept I want to emphasize is that it is very important that these words be spoken out to another person as well so it can be heard and acknowledged. You now have a witness and perhaps this person will help open some insights for you. When you finally do speak of these things you will not only feel good inside but you will begin to heal from the many pieces of shrapnel that may be lodged in your soul. You will become emotionally and spiritually stronger and this comes about by creating balance in all aspects of your life.

Let me encourage you to avoid carrying the burdens of life alone. Professionals like me are always available to listen and guide you through the process and on to many personal victories. This can also be done in a very simple informal way. As mentioned before, group settings are very powerful. There are many people, some are veterans like you, who are not only willing to hear you out but would also benefit by having you listen to them as well. They benefit greatly by you taking the time to hear them and by sharing in the burdens they have carried since coming home from the war. It is a reciprocal relationship and you will both heal more through this process and an honoring will have taken place.

In conclusion, it is important to reiterate that when reflecting on the past and confiding in others it is good to remember that no one can find meaning and understanding for you; it has to be done by you alone. What is inside to be observed and understood can only be approached and addressed by you. When you reach that special place you will know it; and no one else can evaluate or interpret it for you. Your successful healing is a deeply personal thing and the grand finale will always be looked upon in the presence of you alone. However, even though I am encouraging you to reach that finale—that sacred place within yourself—alone, please don't mistake it as an endorsement for not talking to a trusted listener about your experiences. There is something powerfully therapeutic about speaking it out and then having someone acknowledge that they heard what you said; it is the ultimate validation that can set you free from the ties that bind.

9.   The Legacy and the
                        Line of March

Every person's life is a story and no matter at what age that
story continues to develop. As it unfolds we can either be
spectators (mere Observers) or active participants in how our
own account is being written. It's not just where you have been
but where you are going and the incredible thing is that you get
to choose how to write it. (Not to worry though…I'm not insisting
that you to sit down with a pen and paper or laboriously type out
your life's events on a computer. That would be asking too much
perhaps, even though journaling about daily thoughts, activities,
etc., is not such a bad idea. It's just that many of us don't have
the interest.) So this "writing" as I call it, is a metaphor…and I
am talking about structuring your actions, your goals and your
reasons for living each day so that they become mental images
you etch out for the world to appreciate. This is done simply by
how you live. When you do certain things to make a better world

around you it is a way to shape who you are. Doing this each and every day determines your legacy and the process never ends.

So, have you ever stopped to ask, "Who am I?" or "What am I Here For?" "Where am I Headed?" Most of us have kind of asked those questions along the way but find the answers are hard to come by so we don't follow through—usually due to the lack of guidance or suggestions on how to get there. Well, it's important to know the answer to that before you set out to discover who you are (I am writing this to you, the senior veteran, to encourage you to get the most out of the decisions you make because there is a lot of life left to live—and it is never too late to do some personal re-shaping).

To do this "writing" and shaping we can begin by thinking (or actually writing if you are led to do so) about how you feel, what you want and who you love. You can examine your decisions (past, present and future) and this will determine how your life proceeds. Taking inventory about our lives helps us to see life from a better vantage point.

We don't go through life simply making good and bad choices. We go through life making who we are and choice is the hand that does the shaping. To help enhance how you look at tomorrow and all the days to come, I'd like to suggest a plan of action to get everything that you can out of each moment. Why not map out a "battle plan" to direct your life? See if it is something that you like to do. It may also take on an interesting new shape that you enjoy; after all, structure is familiar while serving.

So, back to the question "Who am I?" A simple but surface, answer to that could be just your name and something about your family. But I'm asking you as part of using this battle plan tool to do something different; I'm asking you to reflect a lot deeper than you ever have before about who you are. After all, you need to know where you are right now in order to know where you will be tomorrow. So here's my outline of actions necessary to really know who you are.

Simply ask yourself:

1. What is my story? Your story is more than just a list of events that have occurred during your lifetime. It is all about your self-image and how you truly see yourself. It is contemplating about the things that have caused you to think the way you do today. How did that mindset get there? What is the alternate way of thinking? Your story also can be explained through the memories imprinted on you. They can tell you why certain scenarios happened or didn't happen and that is all part of who you are. Your story is about how you feel, what you want and who you love.

2. What are my expectations? When you become aware of the expectations you have (mostly subconsciously) set up for

yourself, you will begin to see the limits you have put on yourself. Expectations are like sowing seeds that begin to grow into things that we want to gain in life. The problem with that is that many expectations are far below what you are capable of attaining. Contemplate and look deeply at what you expect in life and perhaps reach higher and revamp them. Remember, there is a huge difference between people who expect great things and those who don't.

3.   What is my destination? This is about fulfilling your goals and following certain ways to get where you want to go. Goals for human beings come a dime a dozen; they are endless. And, like a river that flows along and finally empties into an ocean of bigger possibilities, they recycle themselves in the form of condensation. It is most important to envision the end goal...the ultimate fulfillment and keep on that line of march—picking up one foot at a time and walking forward with purpose.

So finally, try to think of this battle plan as using a good tool. Tools are an extension of us and tools make us effective at what we are doing. If we have the right tool we can enhance our feelings of self-worth (probably why power tools or any good tool at the hardware store is so popular with those who have desk jobs. They find that doing something creative with a tool beyond what they normally work with gives them a boost to their self-image and more confidence). The battle planning idea is just that. It's a way to enhance how you feel about yourself on a daily basis. You can simply read it over once a day and give it some thought as you set out on your daily routine or you can be more creative by perhaps even journaling to keep track of what you encounter and have learned along the way. It's just a tool that I now make available to you. I hope it helps.

10.   Epilogue

You did it, you lived through it and you have lived through it all to the end. So our journey into the different aspects of America's aging veterans comes to its conclusion. In summary, it is my hope that by reading this book you have been satisfied and that your life will be better because of it. I enjoyed writing it and through my research have personally gained a new appreciation for all the senior warriors that have sacrificed so much to keep America free.

Since retirement is the grand finale, it is only appropriate to end this book by going over some additional thoughts about it. Earlier we talked about retirement and the many peculiarities that come along with it for veterans. That is where you are. So once again let us do some paralleling of concepts as we reflect back to the time when you were in the war zone and you became a "short timer".

Retirement and being a "short timer" are very closely related. Being a short timer back then meant your moment to return back home and out of harm's way was coming soon. You counted down the weeks, days and minutes before you turned in all your combat gear and boarded a ship or a "freedom bird" to fly back to the United States. In the same respect, I would also say that you probably counted down the minutes and seconds before retiring from your civilian job, especially if your job was not the most enjoyable. Then, when you did retire, another task loomed before you—what to do to fill your time?

Boredom can be a daunting enemy and is an actual side effect of retirement. It causes many people to want to go back to work but it has become increasingly more difficult in today's job market. A case in point for comparison sake: Many Vietnam returnees came home in the 60's and 70's only to re-up for additional tours in the war zone. It was the boredom after the intensity, excitement and importance of what they were doing in the war that led them in that direction.

General MacArthur said in his retirement speech after fifty-two years of military service, "Old soldiers never die, they just fade away." This fading away after retirement has been referenced with regard to just about every profession there is. A soldier is different though. He or she was accustomed to playing a vital role in the everyday lives of other soldiers. Their lives depended upon it and their lives revolved around their unit 24/7. They were part of a team and when they suddenly found themselves without their teammates some had a tendency to become more isolated, alone and very uncomfortable as a form of separation anxiety.

Unfortunately, even the best soldiers eventually have to retire and hang up their gear. At that point, they have difficulty adjusting to no longer being as important as they once were. They may swap war stories with buddies for the first few years but eventually those same buddies move on or begin to die off and are no longer around to talk to. Soon the "fade" begins. I saw this in my dad as he slowly faded away with only the grand memories of being a young virile sailor who was dedicated to protecting what America stood for. As his daughter, I felt sadness at witnessing this process of letting go but thankfully for my father this process came later, especially with his failing health. He could no longer participate in his hobbies and being of service to his family and this was when he finally surrendered to the aging process.

Having a post-retirement plan in place is important; it can mean the difference between happiness and having a hard time adjusting to the change. Here are some tips that can help you ease into the golden years.

1. Establish goals. After working for years, the idea of setting goals can be contrary to your expectations. But goals can give life direction and encourage us to look forward to things in the future. Without that demanding commute and work schedule, you can now substitute a new set of goals

which can be your motivator to get started each day.

2. Donate time or money to the community or your favorite charity. It can feel good and may give you some additional structure and meaning. Volunteering your time can also replace that need to be working, you can set yourself free to do what you love.

3. Start a home-based business. Just because you have retired doesn't mean you have to fully retire. Now may be the opportune time to start a business venture you have always dreamed about, whether it is something hands-on or just being an advisor or consultant.

4. Meet with people. When you get out and do volunteer work or conduct any new business you get a chance to meet people who are not members of your family. Having conversations with different and varied people can stimulate you mentally and you may find that you connect on many levels.

5. Try new things. Part of goal-setting is adding new things to your list. Think of things you've never done before and set a goal to do them. You may discover a new passion. Opening yourself up to endless possibilities is fun and exciting.

People who stop working tend to lose that sense of being part of a team and a connection to something larger than themselves. For example, if you don't show up for work, someone calls looking for you. But when you're retired, nobody comes looking for you if you stay in bed all day. So whether you volunteer, get a part time job or you work in your garden it doesn't matter what you do—it's just important that you do something constructive to fill this void.

When it comes to retirement it is important that each person approach it in a way that is unique for them. I think it's vital to stay connected and to learn new things. When you look at successful people, they generally have been successful because they were willing to do something new. Consider what you would want to do and look for ways to bring you joy. I have always been a major advocate of healing through helping, putting yourself in service to others is a wonderful way to add meaning and purpose to not only your life but those you touch. That is a good way to live life and even better way to wind it down.

It has been a pleasure to write this book. It is important to me not only as a mental health provider but as the daughter of a veteran that I loved dearly. Not a day goes by that I do not think of how wonderful he was and how his life has made me proud to serve the veterans that come into my life.

It is true that books reach many more people than an author ever could in a lifetime. Books become his or her emissary and I'm glad for that. I know you and I have connected in this book and whether we actually meet in person is up to fate. If ever it does happen I will be overjoyed to meet you and give you a personal…"welcome home". Until that day—thank you for your service to our country.

Bridget Cantrell

To order additional copies of this or any other of my
books and for bulk quantity orders contact:

Bridget Cantrell, Ph.D., LLC

1050 Larrabee Avenue Suite 104, PMB 714

Bellingham, Washington 98225-7367

(360) 714-1525

(360) 935-2288 FAX

or

www.BridgetCantrell.com

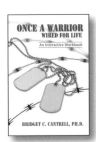

Dr. Bridget Cantrell, LLC

ABOUT THE AUTHOR

Bridget C. Cantrell, Ph.D., NCC, CTS

D r. Bridget C. Cantrell is a noted author, keynote speaker, presenter and counselor in the field of combat trauma, re-integration, family issues, Post Traumatic Stress Disorder (PTSD)/Combat Operational Stress (COS) and Traumatic Brain Injury (TBI). As a leading expert on readjustment and reintegration issues faced by the warrior and then families, Dr. Cantrell's primary work encompasses therapeutic counseling, mental health services and combat trauma workshop presentations to all military service branches including active duty personnel, reservists, veterans, National Guard troops and their family members.

Dr. Cantrell is a Licensed Mental Health Counselor, Certified Trauma Specialist, a Nationally Certified Mental Health Counselor and a member of the American Psychological Association and Association of Traumatic Stress Specialists. She currently works as one of a small number of specially selected and trained Washington State Department of Veterans Affairs

PTSD Contractors.

Dr. Cantrell is the founder and CEO of Hearts Toward Home International, a non-profit organization dedicated to the recovery and reintegration of trauma survivors. Dr. Cantrell's books, *Down Range: To Iraq and Back*, *Once a Warrior: Wired for Life* and *Souls Under Siege: The Effect of Multiple Deployments— and How to Weather the Storm* are comprehensive tools for information and resources on the myriad of transitional issues for returning troops and their loved ones. They are a "must-have" reference addition to your library for any clinical practice, military base community, military family, first responder network, medical practitioner or educator.

Dr. Cantrell has been recognized for her significant contributions to active military and their families throughout the United States and abroad. She is the twice-honored recipient of the Outstanding Female Non-Veteran Award by the Governor's Advisory Committee and the Washington State Department of Veterans Affairs. Dr. Cantrell, along with her co-author Chuck Dean, was the recipient of the prestigious 2008 Erasing Stigma Leadership Award from the Didi Hirsch Mental Health Center in Los Angeles.

Dr. Cantrell travels extensively around the globe teaching and lecturing military personnel and their families regarding the different aspects of re-integration after experiencing war. Her workshops have been given in both the European and Pacific duty assignments. Please contact her directly to schedule a time when she can work with your military unit or organization.

Bridget Cantrell, Ph.D., LLC
1050 Larrabee Avenue Suite 104, PMB 714
Bellingham, Washington 98225-7367
(360) 714-1525
(360) 935-2288 FAX
bc@bridgetcantrell.com
www.BridgetCantrell.com

References

Dean, C. (1999) *Nam Vet Making Peacewith Your Past.*
Seattle, Washington. Winepress.

Marlantes, K. (2011) *What it is Like to go to War.*
Atlantic Monthly Press.

Honoré, R.L. & Martz, R. (2011) *Survival: How a Culture of
Preparedness can Save You and your Family from Disasters.*
Atria Books.

Aging Veterans and Post Traumatic Stress Symptoms, (2007)
http://www.ptsd.va.gov/public/pages/ptsd-older-vets.asp)

Resources

U.S. Senior Vets

http://usseniorvets.com/pension_benefits.html

Toll-free: 877-245-VETS (8387)

VA Non-Service Connected Disability Pension Benefits.

The VA Aid & Attendance & Housebound Pension is designed
to provide qualified veterans and their un-remarried surviving

spouses with financial benefits outside of the traditional VA residential system. This pension benefit, which was established in 1952 under title 38USC, provides a direct, tax free monthly pension to help defray the cost of long-term care.

Eligibility Requirements:

- Must be 65 years old and/or unemployable.
- Must have an Honorable or General discharge (any other than Dishonorable discharge). Must have served at least 90 days of active Federal duty with at least one day during an official period of conflict.
- Must have a medical necessity requiring care.
- Must meet income and countable asset criteria established by the VA.

Department of Veterans Affairs – Vet Centers

http://www.vetcenter.va.gov/

Who We Are

We are the people in the VA who welcome home war veterans with honor by providing quality readjustment counseling in a caring manner. Vet Centers understand and appreciate Veterans' war experiences while assisting them and their family members toward a successful post-war adjustment in or near their community.

Service Organizations

Veterans of Foreign Wars

http://www.vfw.org/

MISSION: To foster camaraderie among United States veterans of overseas conflicts. To serve our veterans, the military and our communities. To advocate on behalf of all veterans.

VISION: Ensure that veterans are respected for their service, always receive their earned entitlements and are recognized for the sacrifices they and their loved ones have made on behalf of this great country.

Vietnam Veterans of America

http://www.vva.org/

Founded in 1978, Vietnam Veterans of America is the only national Vietnam veterans' organization congressionally chartered and exclusively dedicated to Vietnam-era veterans and their families. VVA is organized as a not-for-profit corporation and is tax-exempt under Section 501(c)(19) of the Internal Revenue Service Code.

VVA'S FOUNDING PRINCIPLE

"Never again will one generation of veterans abandon another."

VVA's goals are to promote and support the full range of issues important to Vietnam veterans, to create a new identity for this generation of veterans and to change public perception of Vietnam veterans.

American Legion
http://www.legion.org/

The American Legion was chartered and incorporated by Congress in 1919 as a patriotic veterans organization devoted to mutual helpfulness. It is the nation's largest wartime veterans' service organization, committed to mentoring youth and sponsorship of wholesome programs in our communities, advocating patriotism and honor, promoting strong national security and continued devotion to our fellow service members and veterans.

Disabled American Veterans
http://www.dav.org/

- Made up exclusively of men and women disabled in our nation's defense, the Disabled American Veterans is dedicated to one, single purpose — building better lives for all our nation's disabled veterans and their families. This mission is carried forward by:
- Providing free, professional assistance to veterans and their families in obtaining benefits and services earned through military service and provided by the Department of Veterans

Affairs (VA) and other agencies of government.

- Providing outreach concerning its program services to the American people generally and to disabled veterans and their families specifically;

- Representing the interests of disabled veterans, their families, their widowed spouses and their orphans before Congress, the White House and the Judicial Branch, as well as state and local government;

- Extending DAV's mission of hope into the communities where these veterans and their families live through a network of state-level Departments and local Chapters; and

- Providing a structure through which disabled veterans can express their compassion for their fellow veterans through a variety of volunteer programs.

Military Order of the Purple Heart

http://www.purpleheart.org/

The **Purple Heart** is awarded to members of the armed forces of the U.S. who are wounded by an instrument of war in the hands of the enemy and posthumously to the next of kin in the name of those who are killed in action or die of wounds received in action. It is specifically a combat decoration.

The organization now known as the "Military Order of the Purple Heart" was formed in 1932 for the protection and mutual interest of all who have received the decoration. Composed exclusively of Purple Heart recipients, it is the only veterans' service organization comprised strictly of "combat" veterans.

Make the Connection: Shared Experiences and Support for Veterans

http://maketheconnection.net/resources

Locate Information and Resources:

No matter what you may be experiencing, there is support for getting your life on a better track. Many, many Veterans have found the strength to reach out and make the connection. To find the Veteran resources most helpful for you, fill in your zip code or state below and then check the boxes to indicate the programs or topics you are interested in learning more about.

Association of American Retired Persons (AARP)

http://www.aarp.org

AARP is a nonprofit, nonpartisan organization, with a membership of more than 37 million, that helps people 50+ have independence, choice and control in ways that are beneficial to them and society as a whole.

Geriatrics and Extended Care

http://www.va.gov/GERIATRICS/Guide/LongTermCare/index.asp.

National Center for PTSD

www.ptsd.va.gov

Service for PTSD, Military Sexual Trauma, etc.

Miscellaneous Support

VA Benefits

http://www.va.gov

Women Veterans Program Manager (WVPM):

http://www.publichealth.va.gov/womenshealth/.

National Association of State Women Veteran Coordinators (MVPC):

http://www.naswvc.com

Minority Veterans Program Coordinator:

http://www.va.gov/centerforminorityveterans/

OEF/OIF service members:

http://www.oefoif.va.gov.

Real Warriors:

http://realwarriors.net/forum.

Active Duty, National Guard, Reserves, Veterans & Military Families.

2012 Federal Benefits for Veterans, Dependents and Survivors:

http://www.va.gov/opa/publications/benefits_book.asp.

VHA Office of Rural Health:

http://www.ruralhealth.va.gov.

202 461-1884/461-1928

Transition Assistance Program (online):

www.turbotap.org.

The National Resource Directory (NRD):

http://www.nationalresourcedirectory.gov/

Washington State Dept. of Veteran Affairs:

http://www.dva.wa.gov/benefits.html

Not Alone:

http://www.notalone.com/Site/Default.aspx

Healing Hearts In Hope:

http://www.healingheartsinhope.yolasite.com

Bridget Cantrell, Ph.D., LLC

http://www.BridgetCantrell.com

360.714.1525

Workshops, Books, Support & Counseling: Trauma Recovery for Active Duty Military, Veterans, First Responders and Civilians. Expert Witness Testimony and Consultation.